OTHERS...

Dag Heward-Mills

Parchment House

OTHERS...

First published 2017 by Parchment House
1st Printing 2017

[77]Find out more about Dag Heward-Mills at:

Healing Jesus Campaign
Email: evangelist@daghewardmills.org
Website: www.daghewardmills.org
Facebook: Dag Heward-Mills
Twitter: @EvangelistDag

ISBN : 978-1-68398-192-3

Contents

CHAPTER 1

What You Must Know About *"OTHERS"*

Look not every man on his own things, but every man also on the things of OTHERS. Let this mind be in you, which was also in Christ Jesus:

Philippians 2:4-5

1

Many years ago, a great general of the kingdom of God lived and founded the Salvation Army. He had many leaders and bore much fruit for the kingdom of God. One day, he sent an important telegram to a group of his leaders. He asked that everyone be present for the reading of the telegram. The leaders gathered around for the meeting with great expectation, wondering what the important message was. When everyone was set, they opened the sealed telegram and proceeded to read it to the gathering. They were in for a shock! Instead of a long letter with many instructions, this special telegram had only one word.

Guess what the word was: *"OTHERS"!*

The gathering of the Salvation Army leaders sat there stunned, wondering what to make of the message, *"OTHERS"*! What did William Booth mean by this unusual message? As they sat there quietly thinking about the word *"OTHERS"*, I am sure God spoke to every single one of them. The word *"OTHERS"* is a message to all Christians.

The Message of *"OTHERS"*!

1. The message of *"Others"* is; " *'OTHERS'* exist"!

2. The message of *"Others"* is; "Our minds must be on *'OTHERS'*"!

3. The message of *"Others"* is; "We are to spend our lives for *'OTHERS'*"!

4. The message of *"Others"* is; " We must live for *'OTHERS'*"!

5. The message of *"Others"* is; " We must serve *'OTHERS'*"!

6. The message of *"Others"* is; "We must lay our lives down for *'OTHERS'*"!

7. The message of *"Others"* is; "We must use all the blessings God has given us to care for *'OTHERS'*"!

Four Things You must Remember about *"OTHERS"*

There are four main things that you must keep your mind on when it comes to *"OTHERS"*. If you can remember these four things, you will have the right attitude towards others.

1.   OTHERS NEED CHRIST!

The woman saith unto him, I know that Messiah cometh, which is called Christ: when he is come, he will tell us all things. Jesus saith unto her, I that speak unto thee am he.

And upon this came his disciples, and marvelled that he talked with the woman: yet no man said, what seekest thou? Or, Why talkest thou with her? THE WOMAN THEN LEFT HER WATERPOT, AND WENT HER WAY INTO THE CITY, AND SAITH TO THE MEN, come, see a man, which told me all things that ever I did: is not this the Christ? Then they went out of the city, and came unto him.

John 4:25-30

Always remember that there are many people who need Christ. Millions and millions of people do not know Jesus because the church has failed to think about *"others"*. Most Christians do not think about the fact that *"others"* do not know Christ. They are happy to enjoy Christ in their churches and their wonderful fellowships. Please remember that many, many people do not know about Christ and are waiting to hear the pure gospel preached. There are many who would give their hearts to God if only someone would witness to them. Indeed, *"others"* need Christ!

The woman of Samaria was quick to remember *"others"*. After she was blessed to know Jesus, she thought of all the people in her city that did not know about Jesus. The woman of Samaria is a great example of someone who remembered *"others"*. Most

3

people are happy to receive something good but rarely think about the others who don't have what they have.

2.   OTHERS NEED A SHEPHERD!

And OTHER SHEEP I HAVE, which are not of this fold: them also I must bring, and they shall hear my voice; and there shall be one fold, and one shepherd.

John 10:16

"Other sheep have I!" This means there are many sheep in other places who are waiting for the shepherd. Jesus was constantly aware of other people who needed His shepherding love and care. Jesus was aware of many *"others"* who needed His shepherding and pastoral teachings. Are you aware of *"others"* who need a shepherd and shepherding care?

It is important to remember that many Christians need a shepherd. It is one thing to be saved, and it is another thing to be pastored and shepherded properly.

There is a great need for good shepherds and good pastors. Jesus said, "Other sheep have I"! There are other Christians who are waiting and hoping that a pastor would be raised up to care for them and feed them. Most Christians are happily enjoying their men of God who minister powerfully under the anointing. They enjoy the good preaching and the great ministrations that come to them daily. Because of the good times they have, they forget about others. But there are many others who also need a shepherd. Let us endeavour to raise up more pastors and send them to more towns, more cities and more villages. *"Others"* need shepherds! *"Others"* need churches! *"Others"* need pastors! *"Others"* are waiting for us to train them!

2.   OTHERS MUST HEAR THE MESSAGE!

And he said unto them, I MUST PREACH the kingdom of God TO OTHER CITIES ALSO: for therefore am I sent.

Luke 4:43

If God has blessed you with a good message, always remember that there are others who need to hear your wonderful message. It is a blessing that people like Kenneth Hagin felt the burden to take the faith message to the rest of the world. Many others outside America needed to hear the faith message. I am one of the *"others"* who received Kenneth Hagin's wonderful messages. Kenneth Hagin did not know me personally but I am one of the *"others"* on the fringes who benefitted greatly from his message.

This is why I am burdened to take the message of shepherding, church growth and loyalty to the rest of the world. If God has blessed you with a great message, it is important for you to share this message with as many people as possible. Others need to hear! Others are important! Others must hear the message!

3. OTHERS HAVE ISSUES!

Do not only think about your issues. Think about the issues that affect other people. Many people have diverse problems. Many people have complicated issues that they cannot resolve. Most of the time, we are bogged down by our own issues. We do not lift up our eyes to see how other people are suffering.

It is sad that most Christians do not remind themselves that others have issues. If you, who have two legs and two eyes cannot get a job, then can you imagine how difficult it is for a blind person to find a job?

If you, who have two legs and two eyes cannot get a job, then can you imagine how difficult it is for a cripple to find a job?

It is time to start thinking about *"others"*! What is it like for beggars? What is it like for blind people? What is it like for the handicapped? When you think about *"others"* you will receive the compassion and the grace to help them!

Look not every man on his own things, but every man also on THE THINGS OF OTHERS.

Philippians 2:4

5

CHAPTER 2

"OTHERS" or "SELF"

And he said to them all, if any man will come after
me, let him DENY HIMSELF, and take up his cross
daily, and follow me.

Luke 9:23

Thinking about *"others"*, working for *"others"* and loving *"others"* is a mysterious key to your greatest blessing!

Life is either about you or about others! There is a decision you are going to have to make. Either you live for yourself or you live for others! Living for yourself is a selfish life. It is a life about self-interests, self-love and self-enhancement.

You can decide today that you will care for others instead of just caring for yourself. Living for others and doing things for others produces a richer much more fulfilling life. Jesus Christ told us to deny "ourselves" and follow Him. Saying "No" to yourself is saying "No" to a life of self-centeredness. Saying "No" to self is the beginning of a life that cares for *"others"*.

The Dangers of Self-Centredness and Self Promotion

1.   Self-promotion caused the fall of Lucifer.

You can choose to promote yourself or to promote others. Self-promotion is the deadly sin of satan! Satan exalted himself instead of exalting God and was cast down as a withered branch. From the moment he was cast down, he has been inspiring multitudes to do the same things that led to his destruction. Satan said, "I will exalt! I will ascend! I will sit! I will be like the most high!" He constantly used the word "I" and sought to exalt himself. This was the cause of the fall of Lucifer. Will it be the cause of your fall as well? Thinking only about yourself and not helping others will lead to your downfall.

How art thou fallen from heaven, O Lucifer, son of the morning! How art thou cut down to the ground, which didst weaken the nations! For thou hast said in thine heart, I will ascend into heaven, I WILL EXALT my throne above the stars of God: I WILL SIT also upon the mount of the congregation, in the sides of the north: I WILL ASCEND above the heights of the

clouds; **I WILL BE LIKE the most High. Yet thou shalt be brought down to hell, to the sides of the pit.**

Isaiah 14:12-15

Therefore thus saith the Lord GOD; because thou hast LIFTED UP THYSELF in height, and he hath shot up his top among the thick boughs, and his heart is lifted up in his height;

Ezekiel 31:10

2.   **Self-promotion caused the fall of the first man.**

The serpent said unto the woman, Ye shall not surely die: For God doth know that in the day ye eat thereof, then YOUR EYES SHALL BE OPENED, and YE SHALL BE AS GODS, knowing good and evil. And when the woman saw that the tree was good for food, and that it was pleasant to the eyes, and a tree to be desired to make one wise, she took of the fruit thereof, and did eat, and gave also unto her husband with her; and he did eat.

Genesis 3:4-6

Adam the first man, also wanted to make himself a god. He wanted to become much greater than God had made him. Satan tempted him and pushed him to go higher to experience something greater.

This was satan's temptation to the first man – and it is his temptation for all of us! Throughout your life, you will be offered things God has not given you, you will be tempted to have things God has not given you. You will be tempted with *self-promotion.*

In the Bible, Jesus offers us the opportunity to work for Him so that He can look after us. Seek ye first the kingdom of God and His righteousness and all these things will be added unto you. Unfortunately, we want to seek these things for ourselves instead of allowing God to give them to us.

Many who sought to be elevated financially, have rather been thrown down and are wallowing in financial darkness and great difficulty. Today, many of the people who sought to have their eyes opened are living in darkness. Just as Lucifer was thrown down into darkness and difficulty, many Christians have been thrown into darkness and difficulty because they tried to do it themselves.

Do not bother to promote yourself! Don't try promoting yourself! Man wanted his eyes to be opened! Man wanted to be like a god! Man is constantly making efforts to be like a god but he has rather fallen and become like an animal. Self-promotion is a bad idea! Allow God to lift you up Himself! It is time to help *"others"* rather than helping yourself!

3.   Self-promotion caused the fall of Babel.

And they said, Go to, let us build us a city and a tower, whose top may reach unto heaven; AND LET US MAKE US A NAME, lest we be scattered abroad upon the face of the whole earth. And the Lord came down to see the city and the tower, which the children of men builded. And the Lord said, Behold, the people is one, and they have all one language; and this they begin to do: and now nothing will be restrained from them, which they have imagined to do. Go to, let us go down, and there confound their language, that they may not understand one another's speech. So the Lord scattered them abroad from thence upon the face of all the earth: and they left off to build the city. Therefore is the name of it called Babel; because the Lord did there confound the language of all the earth: and from thence did the Lord scatter them abroad upon the face of all the earth.

Genesis 11:4-9

The men of Babel also wanted to create a name for themselves. They wanted to be famous and powerful. It is a nice thing to be promoted. But self-promotion is not the way! Self-promotion is an evil thing. Don't try to promote yourself!

Self-promotion caused the destruction and fall of the city of Babel. The men of Babel earnestly sought to raise themselves up and make themselves a great name. After reading this book, you must decide to set aside all your ambitions to make yourself great. Look to God to make you great. You cannot do it by yourself. Promotion does not come from the east or the west. Promotion comes from God. Let God lift you up! Think about *"others"* and God will think about you!

For promotion cometh neither from the east, nor from the west, nor from the south.

Psalm 75:6

CHAPTER 3

What Jesus Did for "OTHERS"

Jesus said unto him, Thou shalt love the Lord thy God with all thy heart, and with all thy soul, and with all thy mind. This is the first and great commandment. And the second is like unto it, THOU SHALT LOVE THY NEIGHBOUR AS THYSELF.

Matthew 22:37-39

Jesus came to this world to teach us to love *"others"* the way we love ourselves. All human beings love themselves. But it is time to love your neighbour as well. Your "neighbour" represents the *"others"* of your life. *"Others"* are the people whom God has called you to care for. Notice what Jesus said about *"others"*. He said, love them the way you love yourself!

You can be a person who lives to enhance himself, decorate yourself and improve yourself. That is simply a life of self-enhancement. Or, you can live a life dedicated to helping *"others"*. A life of self-love is the lowest kind of life. Let us follow the teaching of Jesus and begin to love our neighbours.

Seven Things Jesus Did for Others

1. JESUS THOUGHT ABOUT *"OTHERS"*.

The scripture teaches us to think about others. The reason why most people do nothing for others is that we do not think about *"others"*. How many people think about the blind? How many people think about the deaf? How many people think about the souls that are lost? How many people think about other nations? How many people think about those in hospital? We are mostly consumed with our own issues.

To meet someone who even thinks about *"others"* is unusual. You can hardly find Christians who think about orphans, prisoners, mental patients or any other unfortunate category in our society.

Many of those who claim to be making charitable donations and helping society are only trying to get tax exemptions for their companies. A lot of charity work is nothing more than a show. People rarely care genuinely about *"others"*! It is no wonder, that our world is being destroyed, by seven billion self-centred, selfish and greedy human beings who do not care about each other.

Look not every man on his own things, but every man also on the things of **OTHERS**. LET THIS MIND BE IN YOU, WHICH WAS ALSO IN CHRIST JESUS: Who, being in the form of God, thought it not robbery to be equal with God: But made himself of no reputation, and took upon him the form of a servant, and was made in the likeness of men: And being found in fashion as a man, he humbled himself, and became obedient unto death, even the death of the cross.

Philippians 2:4-8

2. JESUS CAME TO THIS WORLD FOR *"OTHERS"*.

When ministers of the gospel prosper, they often forget about *"others"*. Hardly do you find successful ministers of the gospel leaving their teeming flocks of fat and overfed sheep, to look for the lost antelopes and deer in the forest! Most pastors are consumed with the needs of their spoilt and overfed sheep.

They are pre-occupied with having marital get-togethers for those who have been married for one year, those who have been married for two years and those who have been married for ten years.

Most pastors are busy attending to their rich businessmen who are already over-visited and over-attended to. Jesus Christ could have stayed on in heaven where there is peace and prosperity. He did not need to leave the safety of heaven and come to live among the wicked men on earth. But He came! He came from heaven! He came all the way! Today, you can hardly find a successful minister of the gospel going away from his comfortable chair and doing anything for God. We seem to be saying, "Let them go to hell! I don't know why they live so far away! But Jesus was so different. He came for *"OTHERS"*! He went out of His way and came to this earth where we were lost and perishing.

One pastor said to me, "I don't have the calling to go to all those towns and villages that you go to." Indeed, many people feel that they do not have the calling to go to *"others"*. But you do not need a calling to go to *"others"*! You are already called to go to *"others"*! Jesus has already set the example. We sing the song; "I *wanna* be more like Jesus." If you *wanna* be like Jesus, you must do the things He did!

> The thief cometh not, but for to steal, and to kill, and to destroy: **I AM COME** THAT THEY MIGHT HAVE LIFE, and that they might have it more abundantly.
>
> John 10:10

3.   JESUS LOVED *"OTHERS"*.

Most people simply love their husbands, their wives and their children. Some people show great love for their extended families. Some people have a strong and extraordinary love for their tribes. But Jesus Christ loved this whole world full of wicked people. This great love for *"others"* is the exact opposite of the human selfishness which has destroyed our world.

The Church of Jesus Christ is also almost destroyed because of the great selfishness that has consumed the prosperous church. The church has become weak because of its selfishness and self-centredness. Other religions have taken over large sections of this world while the Church of Jesus Christ has been reduced to groupings amongst rich city dwellers.

Hardly do the rich and prosperous churches of our world think about *"others"*. They are so consumed with their own needs that they do not realise that the church is shrinking because of their self-centredness. God so loved the world that He thought about *"others"*. By thinking about *"others"* and loving *"others"*, God has won to Himself many sons and daughters.

> **For God so LOVED THE WORLD, that he gave his only begotten son, that whosoever believeth in him should not perish, but have everlasting life.**
>
> **John 3:16**

4.   JESUS SERVED *"OTHERS"*.

Jesus Christ did not come to be served. He did not come to be waited upon. He did not come to be glorified and attended to. He came to serve! He came to minister to *"others"*! He thought about *"others"* and came from heaven to serve God's love and God's power to us. This is how your life must become. A life of serving *"others"*! Serving *"others"* is the key to greatness!

I know that it is difficult to understand how serving *"others"* can help solve your personal issues. But it does! Somehow, it takes your mind off your minor issues. It opens you up to a real world in which people have diverse and unsolvable problems.

Thinking about *"others"* helps you to put your little problems in the right context. Thinking about *"others"* helps you to cut out complaining and whining about petty things. Thinking about *"others"* makes you see how spoilt you are. Thinking about *"others"*, and serving *"others"* can be one of the greatest things you ever did for yourself.

Even as THE SON OF MAN CAME NOT TO BE MINISTERED UNTO, BUT TO MINISTER, and to give his life a ransom for many.

Matthew 20:28

5.   JESUS LIVED FOR *"OTHERS"*.

For the love of Christ constraineth us; because we thus judge, that if one died for all, then were all dead: And that he died for all, THAT THEY WHICH LIVE SHOULD NOT HENCEFORTH LIVE UNTO THEMSELVES, but unto him which died for them, and rose again.

2 Corinthians 5:14-15

The love of Christ is contagious. Jesus Christ lived for *"others"*. Christ loved *"others"*! That kind of love is what

15

constrained Paul to no longer live for himself. The attitude that Jesus displayed in not living for Himself must greatly motivate us all to no longer live for ourselves but unto *"others"*. From henceforth you must no longer live your life for yourself. You must live your life for *"others"* just as Jesus Christ did!

6.   JESUS HELPED *"OTHERS"*.

How God anointed Jesus of Nazareth with the Holy Ghost and with power: WHO WENT ABOUT DOING GOOD, AND HEALING ALL THAT WERE OPPRESSED OF THE DEVIL; for God was with him.

Acts 10:38

The effort that Jesus made to go around the world doing good to *"others"* and healing *"others"* who were sick, is a great example of our Saviour helping *"others"*.

Jesus Himself was well and not in need of healing, but He went around healing all who were oppressed of the devil. Jesus had a good life, but He went about doing good to people who needed something good.

If God has blessed you with life and health, it is your duty to go about ministering to people who are sick and in need of health. Do not wait until you are sick before you learn the importance of ministering to and praying for the sick.

7.   JESUS DIED FOR *"OTHERS"*!

For this is MY BLOOD of the new testament, which is SHED FOR MANY for the remission of sins.

Matthew 26:28

Jesus Christ died for the whole world. He gave His blood to save *"others"*. After loving *"others"*, living for *"others"*, serving *"others"*, caring for *"others"*, ministering to *"others"* and healing *"others"*, Jesus went one further step and died for *"others"*. What do you do for *"others"*?

Most of us would not even lift a finger for *"others"*. The idea of dying for *"others"* is unthinkable to most of us.

"Why should I die for someone?"

"I don't even want to die for myself!"

"Let them go to hell!" is the unspoken cry of many believers today. They say, "I do not know how people got into their unfortunate state. It is not my fault that people are going to hell. It is not my fault that people are suffering. I didn't cause the problems and I don't see how I am going to solve them."

Many of us think to ourselves, "These ungrateful people do not deserve even five minutes of my time. They will not appreciate all the efforts I make." But Jesus Christ came into the world to save ungrateful people who, mostly, do not appreciate what He has done for them.

He came unto His own and His own received Him not. Jesus died for us. Yet, just a few people have received Him as Saviour. If you think about whether people will appreciate what you do for them, you will never do the will of God. It is time to become like Jesus! It is time to listen to the heart of Jesus and follow how He cares for *"others"*!

CHAPTER 4

A Good Samaritan Cares about *"OTHERS"*

And Jesus answering said, A certain man went down from Jerusalem to Jericho, and fell among thieves, which stripped him of his raiment, and wounded him, and departed, leaving him half dead. And by chance there came down a certain priest that way: and when he saw him, he passed by on the other side. And likewise a Levite, when he was at the place, came and looked on him, and passed by on the other side. But a certain Samaritan, as he journeyed, came where he was: and when he saw him, he had compassion on him, And went to him, and bound up his wounds, pouring in oil and wine, and set him on his own beast, and brought him to an inn, and took care of him. And on the morrow when he departed, he took out two pence, and gave them to the host, and said unto him, Take care of him; and whatsoever thou spendest more, when I come again, I will repay thee. Which now of these three, thinkest thou, was neighbour unto him that fell among the thieves? And he said, He that shewed mercy on him. Then said Jesus unto him, Go, and do thou likewise.

Luke 10:30-37

To care about *"others"* is to notice your brothers who are in need. It is important to see the needs that your brothers have. There are many people who pass by and pretend that they cannot see, feel or understand the needs that you have.

The priest and the Levite saw the difficulties of the man who had fallen into the hands of thieves. When they saw his needs, they passed by on the other side of the road and did nothing to help. It is amazing that we, the religious people, are often guilty of neglecting *"others"*.

The Good Samaritan interrupted his journey because of *"others"*. Most people are not prepared to interrupt their busy schedules or their holidays to help *"others"*. Most people say they do not have money to help, but they always have enough money to go on expensive trips.

The Good Samaritan poured the oil and wine into *"others"*. The Good Samaritan poured the oil and the wine into someone he did not know.

The Good Samaritan stopped in his tracks and poured in the oil and the wine. The oil represents the Holy Spirit and the wine represents the blood of Jesus. The whole world is in need of the Holy Spirit and the blood of Jesus. *"Others"* need the Holy Spirit! *"Others"* need the blood of Jesus!

The greatest need for the world today is Jesus Christ and His precious blood. Nothing can save this world from the damnation it is hurtling towards. Only the blood of Jesus can save the souls of the multitude. The greatest need of our world is not boreholes, running water or electricity. The greatest need of our world is Jesus Christ! The greatest love you can show to others is to show them Jesus Christ.

The greatest need for the church today is the Holy Spirit. The Holy Spirit is the living breath of God in our midst. The Lord thy God in the midst of thee is mighty! (Zephaniah 3:17) It is the mighty presence of God in our midst that avails and achieves anything. God's power is released towards us through the Holy

Spirit. It is God's power that can and will change our lives. One of the only things Jesus taught us to pray for is the Holy Spirit. The Holy Spirit reveals the mighty secrets that will change our lives. I depend on the Holy Spirit every day. I need the Holy Spirit every day. The people who are blessing this world the most are those who pour in the oil of the Holy Spirit. Those who release the power of the Holy Spirit in the world today are the apostles, teachers, evangelists and pastors. They are pouring in the oil and the wine. Apostles, pastors and teachers are anointed by God so that they can minister the Spirit. Ministering the Spirit is ministering the oil into the wounds of the hurting people. "He therefore that ministereth to you the Spirit, and worketh miracles among you, doeth he it by the works of the law, or by the hearing of faith?" (Galatians 3:5).

The Good Samaritan did not give excuses when he had to care for *"others"*. You should listen to the excuses that people give for not caring for *"others"*. You should listen to the excuses that people give for not reaching out to the lost souls of our world. The Good Samaritan did not give excuses to not stop. He did not say, "Who is that worthless fellow lying on the road side. I am sure he must have done something bad to deserve what happened to him." Why are we not stopping and helping those who are hurting and dying by the roadside?

The Good Samaritan risked his life for *"others"*. He went over and risked his life to save the man. The Good Samaritan could have been attacked by those who attacked the unfortunate passer-by. People do not come to your help because there are always risks involved. People do not go on evangelism because there are risks in travelling to foreign countries. People do not go to the ends of the world because it is safer to stay at home. It is time for you to become like the Good Samaritan who risked his life to minister the oil and the wine. When churches arise and minister the oil and the wine, there will be a great revival and a great blessing for all.

The Good Samaritan paid the price to care for *"others"*. The Good Samaritan spent his precious money on "others." The Good Samaritan paid the price to save the lost! It will always cost you something to remember *"others"*. There will always be a price to pay when you want to reach out to *"others"*. Any kind of evangelism and any kind of outreach will cost you something. When you rise up and pay the price to save the lost, you will have started your ministry to *"others"*.

The Good Samaritan did not pretend that he could not see the problem. May God have mercy on us for seeing our brothers in need as we pass by and pretend that we cannot see. Remembering *"others"* and helping *"others"* is walking in the love of God. Remember the second greatest commandment: thou shall love thy neighbour as thyself!

But whoso hath this world's good, and SEETH HIS BROTHER HAVE NEED, and shutteth up his bowels of compassion from him, how dwelleth the love of God in him?

My little children, let us not love in word, neither in tongue; but in deed and in truth.

1 John 3:17-18

As you read this little book, God is making you aware of the needs of *"others"*. Every unsaved person, every blind person, every beggar, every deaf and dumb person, every orphan is a person you are called to help. Do not pass by on the other side as though you cannot see. God is going to use you to touch *"others"*!

CHAPTER 5

Your Judgment Will Be Based on Your Treatment of *"OTHERS"*

But when the Son of Man comes in His glory, and all the angels with Him, then He will sit on His glorious throne.

All the nations will be gathered before Him; and He will separate them from one another, as the shepherd separates the sheep from the goats; and He will put the sheep on His right, and the goats on the left.

Then the King will say to those on His right, "Come, you who are blessed of my father, inherit the kingdom prepared for you from the foundation of the world.

For I was <u>HUNGRY</u>, and you gave me something to eat; I was <u>THIRSTY,</u> and you gave me something to drink; I was a <u>STRANGER,</u> and you invited me in; <u>NAKED</u>, and you clothed me; I was <u>SICK</u>, and you visited me; I was in <u>PRISON</u>, and you came to me.'

Matthew 25:31-36 (NASB)

S alvation comes to us by believing in Jesus Christ and His blood. However, this scripture is clear in showing us that another *"judgment of the nations"* will be solely based on the treatment of less fortunate and handicapped people. Judgment will be based on your treatment of *"others"*.

If your judgment is going to be based on how you treat *"others"*, then you must begin to think about *"others"*.

But I thought people only went to hell because they did not accept Jesus Christ as their personal saviour? Yet, this scripture is showing us that people are being sent into everlasting fire prepared for the devil and his angels because they did not care for *"others"*. I am sure we do not understand everything about eternal judgment. Dear friend, the scripture is clear enough. We need no further encouragement to care for *"others"*. Judgment will be based on our treatment and care for the unfortunate group we are calling "others."

Perhaps you have been thinking that the teaching on *"others"* is a nice Bible lesson on showing kindness. Yes, it is a nice lesson on showing kindness. But it is also going to be the basis for your eternal and final judgment.

Your treatment of *"others"* will be the great measuring rod for your judgment on judgment day. Who are *"others"*? Who are the *"others"*? The *"others"* are the people outside your world. They are the hungry, the naked, the sick, the poor, the thirsty, the strangers and the prisoners.

How you care for the least of people, how you care for the sick, how you care for the poor, how you care for the hungry and how you care for the prisoners will be the basis of your judgment.

"Others" are very important to God. How you treat people who are not so fortunate will be very important on Judgment Day.

I am sure you do not want to hear the words, "Depart from me, wicked servant. I am sure you do not want to hear the words, "Depart from me into everlasting fire." I am sure you do not want to be classified as a goat and sent away from His presence. I am sure you do not want to be cursed and sent into the fire just because you did not treat such people properly.

It is time to be serious about our ministry to the hungry, the thirsty, the strangers, the naked, the sick and the imprisoned!

CHAPTER 6

A Real Apostle Is Sent to *"OTHERS"*

...he fell into a trance, And saw heaven opened, and a certain vessel descending unto him, as it had been a great sheet knit at the four corners, and let down to the earth: Wherein were all manner of fourfooted beasts of the earth, and wild beasts, and creeping things, and fowls of the air. And there came a voice to him, Rise, Peter; kill, and eat.

Acts 10:10-13

Apostles are special servants that God raises up to minister to many people. An apostle will have a vision to care for other people whom no one can see. Notice the vision that Peter had. He saw many *"uneatable"* animals but was told to "kill and eat". This was an outrageous instruction, as Peter could not imagine himself eating so-called unclean animals. God was placing on his heart a vision for the *"uneatable"*, unreachable, out-of-the-way people who need Jesus Christ. Such is the call of God on anyone who is called to be an apostle.

An apostle is someone who is given a burden for people he does not even know. I may never visit many of the churches I am building. I may never go to the places where we are fighting to build churches. Sometimes people ask me why I go to certain places. It is the most natural thing for an apostle to go from city to city to visit churches and to care for people who live far away.

"Apostle" is not a title that you confer on someone because he has been in the church for a long time. An apostle is someone who is sent to care for many people in many different locations. This is why apostle Paul kept travelling to different cities. An apostle is someone who has flocks in different locations and has to care for them.

If God has called you to be an apostle, you can expect to travel to many places.

Paul said that he would spend and be spent for *"others"*. A true apostle will give his life and exhaust himself of all strength in order to fulfil his great mission to the forgotten ones of our world.

One of my greatest struggles has been to get people to think about *"others"*. "Why do we need to go to all these places?", they say. "Why do you have to build churches in all these towns ? Don't we have enough problems in our own country?

Why Zwedru, Ganta, Gbarnga, Bafata, Buba, Gabu, Macenta, Mamou, Gueckedou, Nzerekore? Why do we have to think about Bo, Kenema, Makeni, Daloa, Gagnoa, Parakuo, Sokode and Kara? What on earth are you doing in Opington, Ziguinchor, Springbok, Thohoyando, Ede, Offa, Umtata and Maputsoe?"

Indeed, most ordinary Christians cannot bring themselves to think about *"others"*. It is the call of an apostle to remember *"others"* and drive the church to help them. God has called us to remember *"others"*! We must go to the ends of the earth.

An apostle is constantly trying to train people to remember *"others"*. You will notice how Paul loved and trusted Timothy because he cared for *"others"*. I have many bishops and pastors under me. But my favourite bishops and pastors are those whose minds and hearts are on *"others"*. Because my vision is *"others"*, I naturally find myself gravitating towards those who naturally care for the lost and forgotten ones.

An apostle is very different from a local community pastor. Many ministers basically think about how to minister effectively among the already established churches. They find no difficulty in going to the same people over and over again. They are excited to go to the rich sections of the church whilst the poor and forgotten ones never come to their minds. Such people may have fantastic titles like "Apostle", "Prophet" and "Bishop" but are actually no higher in rank than a local community pastor. A local community pastor is burdened with his local community, city or region. An apostle is given a vision and a burden for the distant and forgotten ones whom Christ died for. When Peter saw a great sheet come down from heaven with all kinds of animals on it, he was being given the burden of a true apostle.

I once visited Chennai in India. I was amazed to find a church dedicated to the apostle Thomas. Apparently, Thomas had travelled all the way from Jerusalem to India to preach the gospel. A church had been built on the site where Thomas was killed. Can you imagine how long and how difficult it must have been to travel from Jerusalem to India in those days? Can you imagine the sacrifice involved in taking the gospel to India in the year AD 50? An amazing feat indeed! Thomas could have stayed on in Jerusalem and praised himself for being one of the twelve apostles of Christ. The authenticity of his apostolic office was confirmed by the great work he did in India. Today, Christians are found mostly in the southern part of India where Apostle Thomas went.

I once visited Malta, an island in the Mediterranean Sea where apostle Paul was shipwrecked. The entire island remembers the visit of the apostle two thousand years ago. His short visit to the island has made Christianity the main religion in Malta today.

I have produced below, seven scriptures which demonstrate the calling of an apostle. These scriptures show the vision, the heart and the work of true apostles.

Seven Scriptures and Seven Characteristics of Real Apostles

1.   **Real apostles are given the *vision* for *"OTHERS"*.**

And he became very hungry, and would have eaten: but while they made ready, he fell into a trance, And saw heaven opened, and a certain vessel descending unto him, as it had been a great sheet knit at the four corners, and let down to the earth: Wherein were all manner of fourfooted beasts of the earth, and wild beasts, and creeping things, and fowls of the air.

And there came a voice to him, Rise, Peter; kill, and eat. But Peter said, not so, Lord; for I have never eaten any thing that is common or unclean. And the voice spake unto him again the second time, what God hath cleansed, that call not thou common. This was done thrice: and the vessel was received up again into heaven . . .

While Peter thought on the vision, the Spirit said unto him, Behold, three men seek thee. Arise therefore, and get thee down, and go with them, doubting nothing: for I have sent them.

Acts 10:10-16,19-20

2.   Real apostles have a *burden* for many *"OTHERS"*.

Brethren, MY HEART'S DESIRE and prayer to God for Israel IS,THAT THEY MIGHT BE SAVED.

Romans 10:1

For I COULD WISH THAT MYSELF WERE ACCURSED FROM CHRIST FOR MY BRETHREN, my kinsmen according to the flesh: Who are Israelites; to whom pertaineth the adoption, and the glory, and the covenants, and the giving of the law, and the service of God, and the promises; whose are the fathers, and of whom as concerning the flesh Christ came, who is over all, God blessed for ever. Amen.

Romans 9:3-5

3.   Real apostles *care* about many *"OTHERS"*.

Beside those things that are without, THAT WHICH COMETH UPON ME DAILY, THE CARE OF ALL THE CHURCHES.

2 Corinthians 11:28

4.   Real apostles must *travel far* to attend to *"OTHERS"*.

And he said unto me, Depart: for I WILL SEND THEE FAR hence unto the Gentiles.

Acts 22:21

5.   Real apostles must *visit many cities* to attend to *"OTHERS"*.

And some days after Paul said unto Barnabas, LET US GO AGAIN AND VISIT OUR BRETHREN IN EVERY CITY where we have preached the word of the Lord, and see how they do.

Acts 15:36

6.   Real apostles *spend and are spent* for *"OTHERS"*.

And I WILL VERY GLADLY SPEND AND BE SPENT
FOR YOU; though the more abundantly I love you, the
less I be loved.

2 Corinthians 12:15

7.   Real apostles *train people* to think about *"OTHERS"*.

But I trust in the Lord Jesus to send Timotheus shortly
unto you, that I also may be of good comfort, when I
know your state. For I have no man likeminded, who will
NATURALLY CARE FOR YOUR STATE. For all seek
their own, not the things which are Jesus Christ's.

Philippians 2:19-21

CHAPTER 7

God Blessed Abraham Because of "OTHERS"

Now the Lord had said unto Abram, Get thee out of thy country, and from thy kindred, and from thy father's house, unto a land that I will shew thee: And I will make of thee a great nation, and I will bless thee, and make thy name great; and THOU SHALT BE A BLESSING: and I will bless them that bless thee, and curse him that curseth thee: and in thee shall all families of the earth be blessed

Genesis 12:1-3

And the angel of the Lord called unto Abraham out of heaven the second time, And said, By myself have I sworn, saith the Lord, for because thou hast done this thing, and hast not withheld thy son, thine only son:

That in blessing I will bless thee, and in multiplying I will multiply thy seed as the stars of the heaven, and as the sand which is upon the sea shore; and thy seed shall possess the gate of his enemies; And IN THY SEED SHALL ALL THE NATIONS OF THE EARTH BE BLESSED; because thou hast obeyed my voice

Genesis 22:15-18

Abraham became a father of nations because of *"others"*. God blessed him so that he would be a blessing to *"others"*. God said, "I will bless you so that all the nations of the world will be blessed because of you."

There is no other reason why God blessed Abraham than for him to be a blessing to all the families of the earth. All the nations of the earth are to receive a blessing because of Abraham.

Through Abraham, Jesus came to the world. Salvation has come to the whole world through Abraham. Abraham has indeed become a blessing to the entire world.

The greatest blessing is for you to become a blessing. When you are so blessed that you can care for others, then you are truly blessed. If your salvation is just to make you and your family happy, then it is a very small blessing indeed!

You have been saved, healed and blessed so that you can go out and be a blessing to others.

The church is sick and powerless against sin, diseases and many curses. Why is this?

The church has failed to do what it is supposed to do. It has failed to be a blessing to the many waiting and lost souls. We were blessed so that we would become a blessing to *"others"*. If you have failed to become the blessing that God has raised you up to be, then you have completely misused and misunderstood the reason for the blessing.

It is a wonder to see how Christians pile up blessings, seeking more and more of the same things. We seek more cars than we could ever drive. We seek more money than we could ever spend. We seek more earthly things than we could ever use. What are we going to do with everything that we have? We should seek His kingdom and seek to help the souls that are lost, dying and hopeless! By doing His great work, we will see His mighty salvation and multiplied blessings in our lives. Do not seek more blessings! Seek to help *"others"*! Seek to do something for the hopeless, distant and forgotten ones. That is the reason for blessings.

God blessed Abraham for one reason. Abraham was God's channel for releasing blessings on this earth. Can you imagine if Abraham had misunderstood God's reason for blessing him? What would have happened to the rest of us?

God always has a reason for blessing people. When God gave the vision of the book of Revelation to John, it was because of the seven churches. It was not for John to enrich himself or to make himself famous. The reason for the blessing is always clear. Jesus said to John, "I am Alpha and Omega, the first and the last: and, What thou seest, write in a book, and send it unto the seven churches which are in Asia; unto Ephesus, and unto Smyrna, and unto Pergamos, and unto Thyatira, and unto Sardis, and unto Philadelphia, and unto Laodicea."

What was the reason for God giving the Revelation to John? *"Others!"* What is the reason for God blessing you and keeping you alive? *"Others!"* What is the reason for God loving you so much? *"Others!"* What was the reason for God blessing Abraham? *"Others!"*

Christ hath redeemed us from the curse of the law, being made a curse for us: for it is written, Cursed is every one that hangeth on a tree: That THE BLESSING OF ABRAHAM might come on the Gentiles through Jesus Christ; that we might receive the promise of the Spirit through faith.

Galatians 3:13-14

You are about to inherit Abraham's blessings! Why would God want to bless you with Abraham's blessings? The answer is very simple. *"Others!"* You will be blessed mightily so that you can become a blessing to *"Others!"*

It is time to stop misunderstanding the reason for the mighty blessings of God in our lives. The mighty blessings are because of *"others"*. We are saved so that we can help to save the world. We are healed so that we can help to heal the world! We are set free so that we can go out and set the masses free! We have prospered financially so that *"others"* will have some of that money! We have a home so that *"others"* can have somewhere to stay! Walk in the proper understanding of the blessings you receive.

The blessing of Abraham will come to you so that you can become a blessing to *"others"*!

CHAPTER 8

Esther Was Celebrated Because She Helped *"OTHERS"*

Then Mordecai commanded to answer Esther, think not with thyself that thou shalt escape in the king's house, more than all the Jews.

For if thou altogether holdest thy peace at this time, then shall there enlargement and deliverance arise to the Jews from another place; but thou and thy father's house shall be destroyed: and who knoweth whether thou art come to the kingdom for such a time as this?

Then Esther bade them return Mordecai this answer,

Go, gather together all the Jews that are present in Shushan, and fast ye for me, and neither eat nor drink three days, night or day: I also and my maidens will fast likewise; and so will I go in unto the king, which is not according to the law: and if I perish, I perish.

Esther 4:13-16

S erving God is about serving others! Esther was favoured, chosen and married by the king. She lived in the king's house and had access to all the privileges anyone could ever imagine. God had given Esther natural beauty and charm. She had a vast wardrobe of clothes she could never wear.

Esther had money, servants, privileges, dresses and shoes. Princess Diana also had a wardrobe that was as large as ten terraced English houses put together. That is what it means to be a queen!

One day, the nation of Israel needed Queen Esther's help. Her own uncle, Mordecai, was the one who contacted her for help.

Esther the queen, who was enjoying great luxuries, was reminded that there were *"others"* living out there in great danger. She was reminded by her uncle that there were other people outside the palace. There were other Jews just like her who were about to be slaughtered.

Initially, Esther hesitated. She felt it was risky to approach the king when he had not asked for her. She explained the rules of the palace to her uncle, Mordecai. Many successful people come up with excuses and explanations about why they cannot help. If you have been a pastor for some time you will get used to the empty excuses of the rich and successful.

The empty excuses of the unwilling sound like a rat chewing nuts in your ceiling. It is a most irritating sound! When people are giving excuses, they seem to think that no one can see through their empty excuses. Mordecai simply warned his niece who seemed inclined not to help. Mordecai's warning to the beautiful and favoured Esther was in five parts.

A Famous Warning to Remember *"OTHERS"*

1.   If you don't help, God will use someone else to help *"others"*.

For if thou altogether holdest thy peace at this time, then shall there enlargement and deliverance arise to the Jews from another place; but thou and thy father's house shall be destroyed: and who knoweth whether thou art come to the kingdom for such a time as this?

Esther 4:14

Watch out if you think you are the only person God can use. God can and does raise up people to supply the needs of the church. Enlargement can come from many other sources.

2. God will use someone else to deliver *"others"*.

For if thou altogether holdest thy peace at this time, then shall there enlargement and DELIVERANCE ARISE TO THE JEWS FROM ANOTHER PLACE; but thou and thy father's house shall be destroyed: and who knoweth whether thou art come to the kingdom for such a time as this?

Esther 4:14

Deliverance can and will come from other sources if you do not help. Mordecai kept mentioning "another place". There is another place from where God can deliver his people. God can raise up somebody from another place. If you do not want to do the work, God will raise up someone from another place to do what you are unwilling to do.

3. You will be destroyed if you do not help *"others"*!

For if thou altogether holdest thy peace at this time, then shall there enlargement and deliverance arise to the Jews from another place; but THOU and thy father's house SHALL BE DESTROYED: and who knoweth whether thou art come to the kingdom for such a time as this?

Esther 4:14

Destruction will come to those who fail to help *"others"*. Mordecai warned Esther about impending destruction to her life if she refused to take a small risk for God's people. Destruction is waiting for those who forget about *"others"*.

This is a warning to those who are asked to help in the work of God.

In spite of all the preaching about prosperity, most ministers are poor. In spite of all the talk about a good life and prosperity, many churches are in debt. Even though they emphasize prosperity, they are destroyed financially because they forget about *"others"*. Mordecai was clear in his warning. If you forget about *"others"* you will be destroyed!

4.   Your family will be destroyed if you do not help *"others"*!

For if thou altogether holdest thy peace at this time, then shall there enlargement and deliverance arise to the Jews from another place; but thou and THY FATHER'S HOUSE SHALL BE DESTROYED: and who knoweth whether thou art come to the kingdom for such a time as this?

Esther 4:14

You were supposed to help *"others"!* The *"others"* are people who are important to God. Just as you neglected the *"others"* who were important to God, God may neglect the *"others"* (your family) who are important to you! Esther was given a strong warning about impending destruction for her family. It is time to stop thinking only about your three children. There are many more children in the world apart from your three biological children. And God cares about them too!

5.   Perhaps, the reason God made you the queen is so you can help *"others"*!

… and who knoweth whether thou art come to the kingdom for such a time as this?

Esther 4:14

There is a reason for everything. There is a reason for your prosperity. You have come to the kingdom with your prosperity for a reason. You were raised up to deliver *"others"*! Many people are irrelevant to the work of God because they do not know why they are around. They strut around in church but they have lost their importance because they are not willing to help solve the problems of *"others"*.

Do not lose your relevance by neglecting the divine reason for which God raised you up. We do not remember Esther today because she was a queen; there have been many queens in the history of mankind. All the kings of Israel had wives who were queens but we do not know any of them. Being a queen is not what made Esther famous. She became famous because she helped *"others"*.

We know Esther and we remember her because of the great work she did in remembering others. She risked her life and she risked her position for the sake of *"others"*. That is why God brought her to the kingdom at such a time.

CHAPTER 9

Moses Became President by Looking on the Burdens of *"OTHERS"*

And it came to pass in those days, when Moses was grown, that he went out unto his brethren, and **LOOKED ON THEIR BURDENS:** and he spied an Egyptian smiting an Hebrew, one of his brethren.

And he looked this way and that way, and when he saw that there was no man, he slew the Egyptian, and hid him in the sand.

Exodus 2:11-12

How many people truly become the head of a nation? How many become the first leader of their country? Most nations have a statue in the centre of the capital city to commemorate their first president. How do people become the first president of an entire nation? By looking on the burdens of the people in that nation!

How do you become great and famous like Moses? Thinking about others is the key to greatness. Thinking about *"others"* is also a key to having a fulfilled life. Your life will be far richer because you think about *"others"*. Almost everyone who became famous did so because they thought about *"others"*. Moses was no exception to this rule. Moses became the first head of Israel because he was concerned about *"others"*.

Even though Moses was living in the Egyptian palace as a relative of Pharaoh, he was concerned about *"others"*. Moses' brothers and sisters were apparently Egyptian princes and princesses. Moses was a member of the royal family. Yet, Moses looked on the burdens of the Israelites.

Unfortunately, most people who are blessed with royalty, luxury and prosperity, forget about the burdens that *"others"* are carrying. It is time to remember *"others"*. By thinking about others and remembering *"others"*, you will rise out of obscurity. Your master key to rising out of obscurity is to remember *"others"*.

You would not know me if I was only thinking about my family. You would not be reading this book if I was only thinking about my church. I already have a church and do not need to know any more people. I am not writing this book because of my own church or family. I am writing this book because of *"others"*. You know about me and you are reading my book because I think about *"others"*. Today, I may not know you and I may not know your name, but you know about me. But if you think about *"others"* and work for others, many people will know about you.

Moses is a good example of someone who rose out of obscurity by thinking about *"others"*. A selfish life is one that enjoys the privileges of luxury and success privately and exclusively. Living in the palace as a member of the royal family in no way blinded Moses to the burdens of *"others"*.

Sometimes, people live in royal marriages and have excellent husbands or fantastic wives. They are enjoying the purple-coloured royalty of marriage. Food is good! Sex is great! Home is amazing! Such people forget that there are other kinds of marriages that are not so exciting. They forget that there are *"others"* who do not have such good fortune in marriage. Many of the people with perfect marriages simply cannot relate with or understand those with difficult marriages. "Pull yourself together," "Take the seven steps to a good marriage," they say. But they simply do not understand difficult marriages because they are stuck up in the realms of royalty. Such people can no longer relate with what happens amongst commoners. It is time to be like Moses. Even if you are up there in the royal palace, you must remember the *"others"* down below.

CHAPTER 10

Nehemiah Became Famous by Thinking about "OTHERS"

The words of Nehemiah the son of Hachaliah. And it came to pass in the month Chisleu, in the twentieth year, as I was in Shushan the palace, That Hanani, one of my brethren, came, he and certain men of Judah; and I ASKED THEM CONCERNING THE JEWS that had escaped, which were left of the captivity, and concerning Jerusalem.

And they said unto me, the remnant that are left of the captivity there in the province are in great affliction and reproach: THE WALL OF JERUSALEM ALSO IS BROKEN down, and the gates thereof are burned with fire.

And it came to pass, WHEN I HEARD THESE WORDS, I SAT DOWN AND WEPT that, and mourned certain days, and fasted, and prayed before the God of heaven.

Nehemiah 1:1-4

The story of Nehemiah and his place amongst the heroes of the Bible, started with his burden for the far away broken walls of Jerusalem. Your rise to fame will begin when you develop a burden for something else apart from your personal life. You will become a national hero when you can bring yourself to stop thinking about your own needs and start thinking about other people's issues.

Thinking about others is the key to having a fulfilled life. Your life will be far richer because you think about others. Almost everyone who became famous did so because he thought about others. Nehemiah was no exception to this rule. Nehemiah became the world famous builder of the walls of Jerusalem because he thought of others. If he had not thought of others, he would have passed away from this world without our ever having known of the name 'Nehemiah'.

Nehemiah was having a good time in the palace of the king of Shushan. He was living in the palace and he had a good job as the cupbearer of the king. Most people would be happy to live on peacefully, thanking God that they had escaped the difficulty of being prisoners of war.

Even though Nehemiah was okay, he was still thinking about others. Nehemiah was so burdened by the broken walls of Jerusalem that it showed on his face. At work, his boss noticed a change in his demeanour.

Wherefore the king said unto me, why is thy countenance sad, seeing thou art not sick? this is nothing else but sorrow of heart. Then I was very sore afraid, and said unto the king, let the king live for ever: why should not my countenance be sad, when the city, the place of my fathers' sepulchres, lieth waste, and the gates thereof are consumed with fire?

Nehemiah 2:2-3

It is time to be burdened and troubled with our backslidden modern church. The spiritual walls of the church are down and there is much desolation all over the church world. Missionaries are not sent out any more! Few people preach about salvation! Unsaved souls are not precious to the average pastor! The church is preaching about money, success and wealth instead of preaching about Jesus Christ and His blood. The defences of the church are down and false religions are taking over territories that were once completely Christianised. When will there be men of God who will be burdened with the broken down walls of the church? A mighty spiritual restoration has taken place in your life when you are burdened with things that do not concern your personal welfare.

Sadly, many pastors are not burdened about the state of the church. You can only care for *"others"* when the burden comes from your heart. When you are troubled from within it is difficult to hide it. It shows on your face. Everyone can see that you are burdened and troubled about something. Unfortunately, many priests do the work of God without a genuine burden for the people.

It is time to care about other churches! It is time to love all the people of God, not just those in your little world!

CHAPTER 11

David Became a "National Hero" by Thinking about *"OTHERS"*

And as he talked with them, behold, there came up the champion, the Philistine of Gath, Goliath by name, out of the armies of the Philistines, and spake according to the same words: and David heard them.

And all the men of Israel, when they saw the man, fled from him, and were sore afraid. And the men of Israel said, Have ye seen this man that is come up? Surely to defy Israel is he come up: and it shall be, that the man who killeth him, the king will enrich him with great riches, and will give him his daughter, and make his father's house free in Israel.

And David spake to the men that stood by him, saying, what shall be done to the man that killeth this Philistine, and taketh away the reproach from Israel?

For WHO IS THIS UNCIRCUMCISED PHILISTINE, THAT HE SHOULD DEFY THE ARMIES OF THE LIVING GOD?

1 Samuel 17:23-26

David became the darling boy of Israel when he served in the king's palace. David then became a national hero by fighting and killing Goliath. How did David become a national hero? How did David go from insignificance to national importance? David became famous because he expressed concern about how the armies of Israel were being treated.

David was not even in the army when he showed concern about the state of the army. When David found out that the armies of the Lord were being taunted and defied, he could not hold back his feelings. His words of concern for the disrespect shown to the armies of Israel were reported back to the king.

One thing led to another and he was sent to fight the battle of his life. Imagine that the famous battle "David and Goliath" came on because a young man was concerned about an army being despised. David killed Goliath and became a national hero because he thought about *"others"*. David was obviously not thinking about his safety. Everyone else was thinking about their own safety and security.

If David had not shown concern for *"others"*, he would have remained an insignificant palace servant. His concern for *"others"* made him unusual! His concern for *"others"* placed him above the ordinary. David's concern for *"others"* elevated him to the highest realms of fame.

Your key to becoming a national hero is to think about *"others"*. Thinking about your own little life will not take you very far. If you are waiting for a time when you will be free of problems so you can think of *"others"* then you will wait forever! Rise up now and start to care about people who are far away. Greatness comes by thinking about *"others"*!

It is time to think about souls! It is time to think about people who do not know Christ and are waiting for salvation! It is time to forget about your own safety. It is time to forget about your own financial security. It is time to spend money on *"others"*. Thinking about *"others"* will make you a national hero.

CHAPTER 12

Joseph Became a "Darling Boy" So He Could Help *"OTHERS"*

And when Joseph's brethren saw that their father was dead, they said, Joseph will peradventure hate us, and will certainly requite us all the evil which we did unto him.

And they sent a messenger unto Joseph, saying, Thy father did command before he died, saying, So shall ye say unto Joseph, Forgive, I pray thee now, the trespass of thy brethren, and their sin; for they did unto thee evil: and now, we pray thee, forgive the trespass of the servants of the God of thy father.

And Joseph wept when they spake unto him. And his brethren also went and fell down before his face; and they said, Behold, we be thy servants. And Joseph said unto them, Fear not: for am I in the place of God?

But as for you, ye thought evil against me; but GOD MEANT IT UNTO GOOD, TO BRING TO PASS, AS IT IS THIS DAY, TO SAVE MUCH PEOPLE ALIVE. Now therefore fear ye not: I will nourish you, and your little ones. And he comforted them, and spake kindly unto them.

Genesis 50:15-21

J oseph was a "darling boy" to his father. Joseph's "darling boy" status generated so much jealousy from his brothers. In the end, all things worked together for good and he became the prime minister of Egypt.

Thankfully, Joseph recognised that his rise to great fame and power was not just about himself but about *"others"*. He could have said to himself, "God has vindicated me and made me the great prime minister of Egypt." He could have said, "God has punished my brothers for their wickedness." But God showed him that his "darling boy" status, his deliverance from slavery and prison and his promotion were actually not for him, but for others. It was all about other Israelite children being saved from the famine.

Thinking about others is the key to having a fulfilled life. Your life will be far richer because you think about *"others"*. Almost everyone who became famous did so because they thought about others. Joseph was no exception to this rule. Joseph was chosen to become the famous redeemer of his wicked brothers and the entire nation of Israel because he would think of *"others"*. It is important to think that your blessings and prosperity are given because of *"others"*.

Just like Esther and Moses, Joseph was having a good time in the palace of the king of Egypt. He was living in the palace and he had a good job as the Number Two in the nation of Egypt. Most people would be happy to live on peacefully, thanking God that they had attained such a high position in a foreign land.

But Joseph had a different mind. He thought about *"others"*. He said, "God has raised me up to save much people alive."

Do you know why God has raised you up? Do you know why God has given you a good position? Do you know why God has given you money?

Be like Joseph! Always remember that God has raised you up because of *"others"*!

CHAPTER 13

Daniel Became a Great Prophet by Thinking about *"OTHERS"*

In the first year of his reign I Daniel understood by books the number of the years, whereof the word of the Lord came to Jeremiah the prophet, that he would accomplish seventy years in the desolations of Jerusalem.

And I set my face unto the Lord God, to seek by prayer and supplications, with fasting, and sackcloth, and ashes:

And I prayed unto the Lord my God, and made my confession, and said, O Lord, the great and dreadful God, keeping the covenant and mercy to them that love him, and to them that keep his commandments;

WE HAVE SINNED, and have committed iniquity, and have done wickedly, and have rebelled, even by departing from thy precepts and from thy judgments: NEITHER HAVE WE HEARKENED unto thy servants the prophets, which spake in thy name to our kings, our princes, and our fathers, and to all the people of the land.

O Lord, righteousness belongeth unto thee, but unto us confusion of faces, as at this day; to the men of Judah, and to the inhabitants of Jerusalem, and unto all Israel, that are near, and that are far off, through all the countries whither thou hast driven them, because of their trespass that they have trespassed against thee. O Lord, to us belongeth confusion of face, to our kings, to our princes, and to our fathers, because we have sinned against thee. To the Lord our God belong mercies and forgivenesses, though WE HAVE REBELLED against him;

NEITHER HAVE WE OBEYED the voice of the Lord our God, to walk in his laws, which he set before us by his servants the prophets. Yea, all Israel have transgressed thy law, even by departing, that they might not obey thy voice; therefore THE CURSE IS POURED UPON US, and the oath that is written in the law of Moses the servant of God, because we have sinned against him.

Daniel 9:2-11

The key to becoming a great prophet is thinking about *"others"*. Daniel, one of the greatest prophets that ever lived, had a great heart for *"others"*. You can always know someone's heart when you listen to his prayers. Thinking about *"others"* will always be master key to having a fulfilled life.

Daniel was a prime minister in different governments. Under Emperor Nebuchadnezzar he was made the ruler of the province of Babylon and the chief of the governors over all the wise men of Babylon. Under Emperor Darius, Daniel was the first of the three presidents. How on earth did he become so great?

Well, Daniel could have lived his life happily because he had such political clout. His high governmental jobs were enough to disconnect him from normal Jewish society. However, your life always becomes richer because you think about others. As I have been sharing, most of the national heroes you know about became great by thinking about others.

Daniel's heart was revealed in his prayer for his nation. Daniel prayed for Israel because he knew that his nation had sinned against God. His prayer is recorded above and you will notice the words, *"We"* and *"us"*. He confessed the sins of Israel as though they were his personal sins. His burden was for the other Israelites. Even though Daniel was having a great time in the palace, he spent his time praying for *"others"*.

Daniel prayed earnestly for Israel. He prayed so fervently that God sent angels to answer his prayers. It is Daniel's burden for *"others"* that distinguished him in captivity. Israel was on his heart! *"Others"* were on his heart! God's people were on his heart! He was burdened with the burden of Israel.

It is not that Daniel did not have personal problems. Daniel and his friends had been castrated. They were eunuchs in Babylon. Indeed, when he asked to have a special diet in the king's palace, he had to seek permission from the prince of eunuchs who was in charge of the eunuchs.

Now God had brought Daniel into favour and tender love with the PRINCE OF THE EUNUCHS. And the PRINCE OF THE EUNUCHS said unto Daniel, I fear my lord the king, who hath appointed your meat and your drink: for why should he see your faces worse liking than the children which are of your sort? Then shall ye make me endanger my head to the king.

Then said Daniel to Melzar, whom the PRINCE OF THE EUNUCHS HAD SET OVER DANIEL, Hananiah, Mishael, and Azariah, Prove thy servants, I beseech thee, ten days; and let them give us pulse to eat, and water to drink.

Daniel 1:9-12

Daniel, Hananiah, Mishael and Azariah were probably having serious erectile dysfunction due to the absence of testicles. He and his fellow eunuch friends must have desired to have normal lives, but their lives were far from normal. In spite of his personal problems, Daniel had a heart for *"others"*. His prayers were not about having a miracle marriage or miracle children. His prayers were about the nation of Israel and their sinful spiritual state.

Daniel is remarkable because he thought about *"others"*. Daniel is remembered today because of his great heart for *"others"*. Daniel is honoured today because even though he had serious personal problems, he still managed to think about *"others"*.

Today, many people are named after the prophet Daniel. Daniel lived thousands of years ago but we all know about him. Today, many people name their children after the prophet Daniel because he was such a great person. I am sure you know several people who are called Daniel, Danny, Dan or Danny-boy! All these people are named after this one great prophet who prayed for *"others"* in spite of his personal problems.

CHAPTER 14

Job Was Healed Because He Prayed for *"OTHERS"*

And THE LORD TURNED THE CAPTIVITY OF JOB, WHEN HE PRAYED FOR HIS FRIENDS: also the Lord gave Job twice as much as he had before.

Then came there unto him all his brethren, and all his sisters, and all they that had been of his acquaintance before, and did eat bread with him in his house: and they bemoaned him, and comforted him over all the evil that the Lordhad brought upon him: every man also gave him a piece of money, and every one an earring of gold.

So the Lord blessed the latter end of Job more than his beginning: for he had fourteen thousand sheep, and six thousand camels, and a thousand yoke of oxen, and a thousand she asses. He had also seven sons and three daughters.

Job 42:10-13

The key to Job's deliverance was his prayer for *"others"*. God actually told Job to pray for *"others"* rather than to pray for himself. When you think about *"others"* and when you help *"others"*, great blessings start coming into your life.

Many people spend their lives praying for themselves, praying for blessings and praying for help from God. Is it not amazing that when God wanted to bless Job and deliver him from his great calamity, He simply asked him to pray for *"others"*?

Job became the most famous survivor of trials that ever lived, because of the heart he had for *"others"*. You can always know someone's heart when you listen to the person's prayers. Praying for *"others"* is a master key to having a fulfilled life. Job was afflicted in many ways. He lost all his children, his businesses, his property, his good health and even his close associates. His wife asked him to denounce God. His friends pointed out that he must have committed some secret sins that attracted such problems.

Job had a great need for personal prayer. Job was the one who was sick. Job was the one who had financial problems and family crises. Job could have spent all the time praying for deliverance from his many calamities. He could have forgotten about everyone else and concentrated on his own afflictions. But he thought of others! He thought about his friends and prayed for them.

Most people become great by thinking about others! Today, Job is remembered as the man who stayed focused on God, even in the most difficult circumstances. Job is the quintessence of endurance and survival! Job overcame many amazing difficulties. How did he do it? How did he pray? He prayed for *"others"*!

Your greatness, your fame and your promotion will come in the day you overcome selfishness and bring yourself to pray for *"others"*! It is time to rise up and pray for *"others"*.

The reason you are unable to pray for a long time is that you do not pray for anyone or anything other than yourself. Honestly, you will not have much to pray for if you are praying for yourself. Your prayers will last for only a few minutes and you will sit there wondering why people pray for a long time.

It is time to rise up and pray for *"others"*. Overcome the spirit of selfishness and self-centredness! Pray for *"others"*! Intercede for *"others"*! Do something for *"others"*!

CHAPTER 15

The Four Lepers *"Did Well"* Because They Remembered *"OTHERS"*

And there were four leprous men at the entering in of the gate: and they said one to another, why sit we here until we die? If we say, we will enter into the city, then the famine is in the city, and we shall die there: and if we sit still here, we die also. Now therefore come, and let us fall unto the host of the Syrians: if they save us alive, we shall live; and if they kill us, we shall but die.

And they rose up in the twilight, to go unto the camp of the Syrians: and when they were come to the uttermost part of the camp of Syria, behold, there was no man there. For the Lord had made the host of the Syrians to hear a noise of chariots, and a noise of horses, even the noise of a great host: and they said one to another, Lo, the king of Israel hath hired against us the kings of the Hittites, and the kings of the Egyptians, to come upon us.

Wherefore they arose and fled in the twilight, and left their tents, and their horses, and their asses, even the camp as it was, and fled for their life. And when these lepers came to the uttermost part of the camp, they went into one tent, and did eat and drink, and carried thence silver, and gold, and raiment, and went and hid it; and came again, and entered into another tent, and carried thence also, and went and hid it.

Then they said one to another, WE DO NOT WELL: this day is a day of good tidings, and we hold our peace: if we tarry till the morning light, some mischief will come upon us: now therefore come, that we may go and tell the king's household.

2 Kings 7:3-9

The story above tells us about the most famous lepers in Israel. How did they become the most famous team of lepers in the Bible?

These four lepers are famous because they thought of *"others"*. If they had not thought of *"others"*, they would have passed away from this world without us ever having known about them.

The four lepers were having a good time eating all the food they had not had for weeks. Suddenly it occurred to them that there were *"others"* in the city, who were hungry too.

The four lepers had experienced the great blessings of abundance. The four lepers were no longer poor. They had it all! They were no longer waiting for a miracle. They had their miracle in their hands. They were no longer suffering or dying. They were walking in unbelievable blessings. But they were about to make the mistake of forgetting about *"others"*. To forget about *"others"* is to make the biggest mistake of your life! They aptly said, "We do not well" if we do not remember *"others"*.

Can't you think of many people who are not *"doing well"* in their businesses, their lives and their jobs? The four lepers realized that they were about to descend into that state of *"not doing well"*. There is no need to descend into that state of not *"doing well"*. There is no need to fall back! You can do well in life, in business and in ministry! These four lepers in the scripture had the key to *"doing well"*. Their key to *"doing well"* was to remember *"others"*.

Many pastors are not doing well in the ministry, because they do not remember *"others"*. Many pastors simply live for themselves and their little community church. They cannot lift up their eyes to see the waiting harvest fields that have been neglected because of their selfishness.

False religions are taking over entire regions as the church concentrates on itself. Churches no longer have salvation altar calls, crusades, breakfast meetings, outreaches, concerts, door-to-door evangelism, person-to-person evangelism or soul-to-soul evangelism. Many prayer meetings are packed with Christians fasting and praying for their personal needs.

You will hear Christians crying and wailing to the Lord at prayer meetings. If you go a little closer, you will hear the topics for yourself. You will find out that almost everyone is praying for himself.

"O God, help this marriage of mine. O God, give me this contract. O God, I want to marry this year. O God, I claim a set of twins before December. O God, I declare that the wealth of the sinner is transferred into my hands. O God, send the angel of wealth into my family. O God, destroy my landlord's evil intention of raising the rent."

In spite of these packed prayer meetings the blessings are not flowing, as they ought. Why is that? God does not bless us so that we will multiply silver and gold to ourselves. He blesses us so that we will be a blessing to *"others"*.

He blessed the four lepers so that they would tell the others that there was lots of food. He blessed the four lepers so that they would transmit the news to *"others"*. Even those four lepers knew that they would not *"do well"* if they did not tell the news.

How can we expect to do well if we do not tell the good news of Jesus Christ to the whole world? How can we expect the wealth of the world to come into our hands if we do not transmit the message that has been entrusted to us?

Many churches are not doing well because they do not remember *"others"*. The key to doing well is to remember *"others"*. The key to doing well is the key of remembering *"others"*. Remembering *"others"* opens the door to prosperity.

Thinking about *"others"* is the key to having a fulfilled life. Your life will be far richer because you think about others. The four lepers did well because they remembered *"others"*! You will begin to do well when you remember *"others"*.

CHAPTER 16

Gideon Became a Judge by Thinking about *"OTHERS"*

And there came an angel of the Lord, and sat under an oak which was in Ophrah, that pertained unto Joash the Abiezrite: and his son Gideon threshed wheat by the winepress, to hide it from the Midianites. And the angel of the Lord appeared unto him, and said unto him, The Lord is with thee, thou mighty man of valour.

And Gideon said unto him, Oh my Lord, if the Lord be with US, WHY THEN IS ALL THIS BEFALLEN US? And where be all his miracles which our fathers told US of, saying, did not the Lord bring US up from Egypt? But now the Lord hath forsaken US, and delivered US into the hands of the Midianites.

Judges 6:11-13

When the angel of the Lord came to Gideon, he complained about what had befallen everyone and not just what had befallen him personally.

Gideon is the most famous judge who ever lived. He judged Israel for forty years. How many judges do you know? Judges hardly make the headlines. Gideon rose to the heights of world fame by thinking about *"others"*. Thinking about others was Gideon's key to having a fulfilled life. Your life will be far richer because you think about *"others"*. Almost everyone who became famous did so because he thought about *"others"*.

Gideon was no exception to this rule. Gideon became the famous warrior who delivered Israel from the Philistines. Many people today are named after him. Personally, I know a number of people called Gideon. Do you think anybody would have been named after Gideon if he had not thought of *"others"*? He would have passed away as another non-entity.

Today, the church is filled with many narrow-minded non-performers who only think about themselves. They say, "Why has this happened to me? Why don't I have this? Why don't I have that? When am I going to have this? When am I going to have that?" It's all about "me", "myself" and "I". Gideon spoke about *"US"*. Gideon wanted *"US"* to be saved. Gideon wanted *"US"* to be healed.

When you think about *"others"* you will be famous in whatever profession you choose. Gideon was a judge and he became the most famous judge of all time because he thought about *"others"*!

CHAPTER 17

Nabal Died Because He Did Not Remember *"OTHERS"*

And David heard in the wilderness that Nabal did shear his sheep. And David sent out ten young men, and David said unto the young men, Get you up to Carmel, and go to Nabal, and greet him in my name: And thus shall ye say to him that liveth in prosperity, Peace be both to thee, and peace be to thine house, and peace be unto all that thou hast.

And now I have heard that thou hast shearers: now thy shepherds which were with us, we hurt them not, neither was there ought missing unto them, all the while they were in Carmel. Ask thy young men, and they will shew thee. Wherefore let the young men find favour in thine eyes: for we come in a good day: give, I pray thee, whatsoever cometh to thine hand unto thy servants, and to thy son David. And when David's young men came, they spake to Nabal according to all those words in the name of David, and ceased.

And Nabal answered David's servants, and said, WHO IS DAVID? AND WHO IS THE SON OF JESSE? THERE BE MANY SERVANTS NOW A DAYS THAT BREAK AWAY EVERY MAN FROM

HIS MASTER. SHALL I THEN TAKE MY BREAD, AND MY WATER, AND MY FLESH THAT I HAVE KILLED FOR MY SHEARERS, AND GIVE IT UNTO MEN, WHOM I KNOW NOT WHENCE THEY BE? So David's young men turned their way, and went again, and came and told him all those sayings.

1 Samuel 25:4-12

Some people have a proud attitude towards *"others"*. It is important not to look down on anyone. Prisoners, handicapped people, the blind, the deaf, the maimed, the sick, the homeless, the hungry, foreigners, widows, orphans and the unfortunate are all precious to God.

The church, God's people, Christians, pastors and God's servants are also precious to God. You must be careful when dealing with these groups of people.

Nabal's attitude towards David's servants reveals an unfortunate attitude towards *"others"*.

David simply asked Nabal to remember him and his men in the day of his prosperity. He reminded Nabal that he had come in a time when everything was wonderful and working well. "Please give us a very small percentage of your wealth so that the men who have helped you so much over the last few months can have a little meal."

But Nabal's answer was laced with a harsh, unfeeling and arrogant attitude.

"Who is David?" he asked.

There are many rebellious and worthless fellows out there!

How can I take my bread, water and meat and give it to a group of stupid and irrelevant people.

To Nabal, *"others"* were stupid and unimportant people. But Nabal was wrong! Nabal was the fool! Nabal was the worthless and rebellious man of Belial. That was his wife's testimony about him. His wife called him a fool. It is important for wives to make an accurate diagnosis about the man they are married to. Indeed, it is important for all spouses to come to a proper and accurate assessment of the person they are married to. This will help you to deal wisely and appropriately with the person you are married to.

And when Abigail saw David, she hasted, and lighted off the ass, and fell before David on her face, and bowed herself to the ground, And fell at his feet, and said, Upon me, my lord, upon me let this iniquity be: and let thine handmaid, I pray thee, speak in thine audience, and hear the words of thine handmaid. Let not my lord, I pray thee, REGARD THIS MAN OF BELIAL, EVEN NABAL: FOR AS HIS NAME IS, SO IS HE; NABAL IS HIS NAME, AND FOLLY IS WITH HIM: but I thine handmaid saw not the young men of my lord, whom thou didst send.

1 Samuel 25:23-25

Nabal died because he failed to help *"others"*. God struck him down and gave his wife to someone else. It is important not to see others as worthless and stupid people.

It is important to see others as important people God has sent you to. It was Nabal who was a drunkard and who destroyed his life through drinking. He had the arrogance to call others worthless and rebellious people. Nabal was shocked when he discovered that he was the big fool.

And Abigail came to Nabal; and, behold, he held a feast in his house, like the feast of a king; and Nabal's heart was merry within him, for he was very drunken: wherefore she told him nothing, less or more, until the morning light. But it came to pass in the morning, when the wine was gone out of Nabal, and his wife had told him these things, that HIS HEART DIED WITHIN HIM, and he became as a stone.

1 Samuel 25:36-37

There is no need to die because you forget *"others"*! *"Others"* are important to God. You will live because you honour others. You will be blessed because you remember *"others"*. You will prosper because you remember *"others"*. You will become a "darling boy" because you remember *"others"*. You will become a national hero because you remember *"others"*.

This book is God's revelation to you about *"others"*. God is showing you what is important to Him! God is showing you how your life will be transformed just by thinking about *"others"*. [77]God is showing you that the way to greatness, fame and honour is by remembering, helping and caring for *"others"*!